The Right Thing to Do

written by Teresa Chi

illustrated by Ashley Lucas

The Right Thing to Do

ISBN: 1500168793
ISBN-13: 978-1500168797

For the toddlers of Redbud Room

When you're shopping and you really want a toy,

and you scream and cry and make LOTS OF NOISE,

that's not the right thing to do.

When an auntie pinches your cheek,

you might throw yourself on the floor AND FREAK,

but that's not the right thing to do.

When you know it's a cold and snowy day,
but you want to wear shorts anyway,

that's not the right thing to do.

When another kid wants to use the red,
you might yell at them to use the blue instead.

But that's not the right thing to do.

The right thing to do is what you should choose.

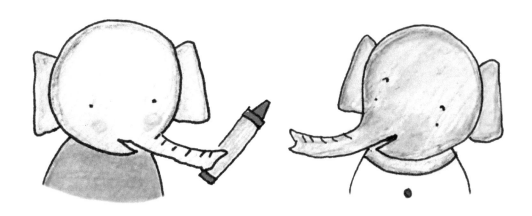

It's all up to you! What will you do?

When it's not your turn to go on the swings,
it's important to wait patiently,

because that's the right thing to do.

When you pass gas, the room starts to smell.
It happens. Remember to excuse yourself!

That's just the right thing to do.

When you don't like what you see on your plate,

try a little bit of veggies, just a taste,

YUM!

because that's the right thing to do.

When the lights are out, it's time to go to sleep.
So close your eyes. Relax yourself, even your feet!

That's just the right thing to do.

The right thing to do is what you should choose.

It's all up to you...

What will you do?

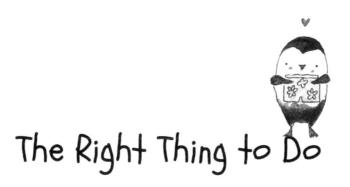

The Right Thing to Do

When you're shopping and you really want a toy
And you scream and cry and make lots of noise
That's not the right thing to do
When an auntie pinches your cheek
You might throw yourself on the floor and freak
But that's not the right thing to do

When you know it's a cold and snowy day
But you want to wear shorts anyway
That's not the right thing to do
When another kid wants to use the red
You might yell at them to use the blue instead
But that's not the right thing to do

The right thing to do is what you should choose
It's all up to you! What will you do?

When it's not your turn to go on the swings
It's important to wait patiently
'Cause that's the right thing to do
When you pass gas the room starts to smell
It happens, remember to excuse yourself
That's just the right thing to do

When you don't like what you see on your plate
Try a little bit of veggies, just a taste
'Cause that's the right thing to do
When the lights are out it's time to go to sleep
So close your eyes, relax yourself, even your feet
That's just the right thing to do...
It's just the right thing to do!

The right thing to do is what you should choose
It's all up to you! What will you do?
The right thing to do is what you should choose
It's all up to you! What will you do?

 # Meet Teresa & Ashley!

Teresa Chi is a Montessori teacher and musician (and now author!) living in New York City. Some of her favorite things are roller coasters, the Beatles, coffee, taking walks in Central Park, and beach days. Teresa likes to practice getting over her stage fright by performing at open mic events around NYC, but her venue of choice is circle time. **The Right Thing to Do** is her fifty-sixth song and her first book.

Ashley Lucas is an illustrator, crafts designer and the self proclaimed 'queen of cute characters'. She is the author and illustrator of various picture books such as 'Boo, Bat & Pumpkin Throw a Party' and the 'I Love New York City Food' coloring book. She teaches private lessons and workshops to wonderfully creative children that make her laugh. She loves animals, art supplies and a good meal out!

Visit Us Online!

Download "The Right Thing to Do"
and listen to many more songs at
www.soundcloud.com/26songs

For fun music activities, please visit
www.teresachi.com

Follow 26songs **on Facebook and Twitter**
to get the latest on what I'm writing about!

♪ Teresa

Love the cute animals in this book?

www.ladylucas.com

cupcakesandowls.blogspot.com

www.facebook.com/purplebatwithredshoes

www.etsy.com/shop/LadyLucasStore

xo Ashley

Bear's Town

MAIL

SCHOOL

LIBRARY

CPSIA information can be obtained
at www.ICGtesting.com
Printed in the USA
LVHW07n0433150518
577223LV00002B/13/P